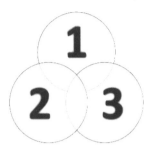

SOCIAL MEDIA
FIELD GUIDE

Volume I

Media Maverix Marketing

www.mediamaverix.ca

TheTop10 Group Corp.
80 Aberdeen Street
Ottawa, ON, K1S 4M7
Canada
Tel.: 613-435-8671
caroline@thetop10.ca
www.thetop10.ca

ISBN 978-0-9917689-0-5

Contents

Forward

My name is Doug Smith, author of Thriving in Transition and The Trauma Code. In 1994 I was immersed in the internet and my early work as a pioneer lead to an executive position with a National Internet Service Provider. My 19 years of experience has given me a respect for and awareness of the power of today's communications capability. Social Media is a new dimension and I strongly encourage you to build a strong foundation of knowledge before rushing in.

The internet is now an extension of the human mind and the opportunity with social media is limited only by your creativity and business savvy; two things which do not usually reside inside just one mind. At the time of this printing in 2012 I have over 6 years' experience immersed in social media and social networks and during this time I have written 3 books on change, transition and performance. I am honored to share my feelings about the *1, 2, 3, Social Media Field Guide*, my personal experience of getting to know the author Caroline Risi, her team at Media Maverix and the performance advantage this document provides you.

Networking, connecting and relating to other people is an art and when I first met Caroline at an Indonesia-Canada event it was obvious she was an artist in relationship building.

Unlike most, Caroline was interested in first, how to expand and monetize Doug Smith's capacity and to fill his sales funnel. She was sincerely interested in knowing me, my history and what my purpose was. She demonstrated her awareness that social media is fluid and strategy is important, but to succeed, people needed to get out there and learn; sometimes by making mistakes. As a former professional athlete, this resonated with my personal journey to the National Hockey League and all of the times I fell down and got back up again.

The social media engine behind www.DougSmithPerformance.com was built by Caroline's team and it helped my internet presence perform better. Through continued effort, my web presence was now putting money in my bank account and I had reached my goal to achieve twenty ways for people to connect with me with just one click. Up to 50 people in a day would connect on social networks and through my website.

This is a simple yet powerful tool for every business yearning to improve and measure their social media performance. I encourage you to invest in your future by taking Steps 1, 2 and 3. Your business will be thankful you did.

Doug Smith CCF
President, DSE Network Publishing
Author of Thriving in Transition
Author of The Trauma Code
www.DougSmithPerformance.com

Introduction

This guide is about making connections and making money.

There are three major components that need to be considered when taking your business and marketing plans online:

1. Benchmarking your current business so that you have a baseline from which to be able to measure your success.

2. Making sure you have a clear goal for your online communication plan to achieve and an equally clear structure for it to follow.

3. Engaging yourself and your network or audience in activities that will build trust, efficacy, ethics, social responsibility, loyalty and action.

There has been a shift in the world of marketing. If you think about it, social media is different; with the introduction of Web 2.0, it's no longer a monologue — it's a dialogue. Your advertising and marketing need to be interactive going forward. Any online product needs to follow the same principal. If you keep this in mind, your success will be solid.

The History of the Internet

1838   Samuel F. B. Morse demonstrates the electric telegraph for the first time.

1843   The U.S. Congress funds an experimental line between Baltimore and Washington, D.C.

1848   Morse's partner, Alfred Vail, wired to the U.S. Capitol to say that Henry Clay had been nominated at his party's national convention. This was the first news dispatched by electric telegraph.

1851   Western Union begins business.

1861   Western Union builds its first transcontinental telegraph line.

1876   Alexander Graham Bell invents the telephone. His first words over it: "Mr. Watson, come here, I want to see you."

1877   Bell Telephone Company is formed.

1885   AT&T is formed to manage Bell's long-distance business.

1913   Western Union introduces multiplexing, the process of transmitting eight messages simultaneously over a single wire (four in each direction).

1936   Western Union introduces Varioplex; now a single wire can carry 72 transmissions at the same time (36 in each direction).

1959   Western Union introduces its Telex teleprinter exchange (hence "telex") service in the U.S.

The 1970s

1972   The Advanced Research Projects Agency becomes DARPA after adding "Defense" to its name. DARPA is a leader in the call for a global network.

1974   The term "Internet" is adopted.

        The X.25 protocol forms the basis of the SERCnet network connecting British academic and research sites, which later becomes the Janet network.

1978   The General Post Office (in the U.K.), Tymnet (in the U.S.) and Western Union International collaborate to create the International Packet Switched Service (IPSS), the first network of its kind.

The 1980s

1981   The network created in 1978 now covers Europe, the U.S., Canada, Hong Kong and Australia.

1989   Tim Berners-Lee connects hypertext with the Internet and personal computers, resulting in the World Wide Web.

The World, based just outside of Boston, begins selling dial–up access to the public, becoming the first commercial Internet service provider (ISP)

The 1990s

1990   The network created in 1978 now provides worldwide networking infrastructure.

The first search engine, Archie, is created at McGill University in Montreal.

1991   Wide Area Information Servers (WAIS), a text-searching system, and Gopher, a document distribution, search and retrieval protocol, are introduced.

1993   The Mosaic web browser is created at the University of Illinois, funded by the *High Performance Computing Act of 1991* (aka the Gore Bill).

1994   Netscape Navigator supersedes Mosaic.

Search engine WebCrawler is introduced.

1995   Search engines/web directories Yahoo! and AltaVista are founded.

1998   Google is founded; relevancy ranking of the web begins.

2000 and beyond

2007   Over a billion people now enjoy access to the web.

2011   It's estimated that 22 percent of the world's population surfs the Internet regularly.

2012   Social media has taken the world by storm. A report from eMarketer found that one in five people around the world will be active on social networks this year. At the end of 2011, 17.3 percent of global consumers regularly accessed Facebook, Twitter or some other platform, and that figure will reach 20.4 percent by the end of the year.

The Future of the Internet

Well, I am not fortune-teller, but here is what five web and computer pioneers had to say in recent years on what the Internet of the future and its associated technology would look like:

Steve Case, co-founder of AOL

In 2010, Case had this to say: "I think that it will continue to evolve. In 25 years it has gone from a first phase, which was really a pick and shovel phase, to simply building the basic platform, the basic technology, the basic network, the basic tool to do well. The second 10 years really was about expansion and really taking it to the mainstream. And...the last few years, and I think the coming decade really, will be about — now that the Internet really is ubiquitous, people are relying on it in increasingly habitual kind of ways — how do you not just create Internet businesses, but create businesses that can impact every aspect of people's lives using the Internet as a tool."

Ryan Ozimek, CEO of PICnet

 When asked about it in 2010, Ozimek said, "I think what I'm excited about and where I see the future of the Internet going is more mobile, more focused on the cloud, and more about building really easy-to-use platforms that people can use to build the next generation of software that hasn't even crossed our minds yet."

Dries Buytaert, creator of Drupal

 "Initially people added a blog to their main website," said Buytaert in 2010. "I think the future is much more integrated, where social is part of everything you do, every website."

And what of the technology needed to power and access the Internet? Two pioneers weigh in:

Steve Jobs, co-founder of Apple

 Apple waged a high-profile war on Adobe Flash, excluding support for the format in its "iDevices," leading to much criticism. In April 2010, the iPad launched without Flash support, and skeptics said it meant the device couldn't properly serve up much of the Internet, as many sites use Adobe's proprietary format. When Jobs was asked a few months later at AllThingsD's D8 conference whether this crippled the iPad, he said:

"Well you know, I'd say two things. Number one: Things are packages of emphasis. Some things are emphasized in a product, some things are not done as well, some things are chosen not to be done at all in a product....

"We're going to instead focus our energy on these technologies, which we think are in their ascendancy and we think are gonna be the right technologies for customers. And if we succeed, they'll *buy* them. And if we don't, they *won't*."

In the case of the iPad and Flash, HTML5 is the technology that Apple touted as the superior format, with Microsoft soon joining in on the Flash bashing.

Bill Gates, co-founder and chairman of Microsoft

In 2011, as the personal computer turned 30, PCMag asked Gates for his thoughts on the PC, which Microsoft's Windows operating system had long since become synonymous with. This is what he had to say about the past, present and future of this, the most significant innovation in personal computing:

"On a societal level, technology will contribute to solving many of our greatest challenges. In global health, it will advance scientific discovery, diagnostics and delivery of health services to the world's poor. In education, it has the potential to ignite student interest in learning and help teachers understand what's working and what's not in the classroom. And in many other areas, computers already are and will continue to be an essential tool for data collection, analysis, and innovation....

"The next 30 years are going to be equally remarkable as the last 30. We're really still just at the beginning of what's possible."Social Statistics

Did you know...?

- Weekly Internet usage has overtaken TV viewing in Canada. In 2010, the weekly average time dedicated to watching TV was outstripped by the time spent online.

- Twenty percent of all the page views on the Internet are on Facebook.

- Twitter averages about 175 million tweets per day

- Pinterest hit 10 million monthly unique visitors quicker than any other site, making it the fastest-growing site ever.

- LinkedIn grows at a rate of about two new members every second.

- YouTube handles 10 percent of the Internet's traffic.

- Google+ gains about 625,000 new users per day.

• In 2011, 82 percent of the world's Internet population over the age of 15 was a member of a social networking site.[1]

Why We Need Social Media

Social marketing has become the necessary evil that once was the newspaper, direct mail or radio.

---

[1] Google Search www.google.com

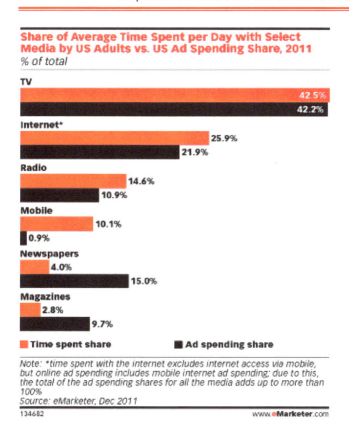

Share of Average Time Spent per Day with Select Media by US Adults vs. US Ad Spending Share, 2011
% of total

TV
42.5%
42.2%

Internet*
25.9%
21.9%

Radio
14.6%
10.9%

Mobile
10.1%
0.9%

Newspapers
4.0%
15.0%

Magazines
2.8%
9.7%

■ Time spent share   ■ Ad spending share

Note: *time spent with the internet excludes internet access via mobile, but online ad spending includes mobile internet ad spending; due to this, the total of the ad spending shares for all the media adds up to more than 100%
Source: eMarketer, Dec 2011

134682   www.eMarketer.com

Figure 1 Share of time spent versus share of ad spending

It is time our spending allocation was adjusted to create the biggest impact based on where our ready buyers are. Internet and mobile spends are nowhere close to where they need to be to capture the audience needed to make the impact required.

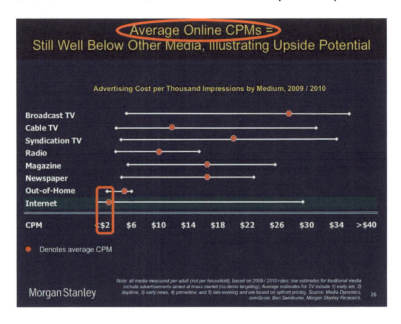

Figure 2 Advertising cost per 1,000 impressions by medium

If we compare reach for dollar, take a guess which medium reaches more people for the least amount of money. (Not that I needed to point this out; I'm sure you already knew this.) So why do we need social media networking in our marketing mix? Well, if implemented correctly and targeted properly, your expenses will go down and your revenues will go up. Can you think of better reasons?

Measuring Social Media Success

Benchmark for a Point of Reference

Why Benchmarking Is Important

Benchmarking provides a baseline measurement to refer to the progress of the different variables over time to see if there is any improvement and is therefore essential for tracking success. If you are implementing social media into your marketing mix or hiring a company to do it for you, recording social media benchmarking measurements before implementing the social media marketing tactics is *vital* in measuring whether progress is being made.

There are a whole range of tools, both free and paid, to measure most elements of your blog-, Twitter- and Facebook-related traffic and statistics.

Five Tools to Measure Your Social Media Success

Blog Measurement

The key element that you should be measuring is traffic to your website. But along with this core statistic, there is a range of other important numbers to keep your eye on:

- Top posts.

- Top referrers.

- What your visitors are clicking.

- Top search engine terms that bring people to the site.

Tool 1: WordPress Statistics

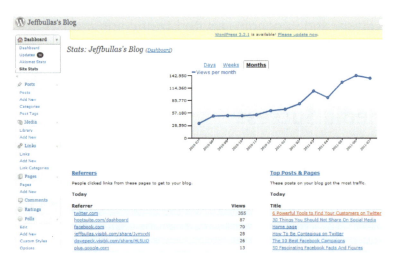

Figure 3 WordPress stats for Jeff Bullas's blog

There are several free plug-ins (including the official one, WordPress.com Stats) available to users that measure and compare topline statistics. These provide a reference to ensure that you are improving and making progress. If we look at the stats for Jeff Bullas's blog in Figure 3 above and take July 2010 as his benchmark, it is obvious that in July 2011 some progress had been made with a few more days to go.

Tool 2: Google Analytics

Figure 4 Google Analytics stats for Jeff Bullas's website

Google Analytics (*www.google.com/analytics*) is another free tool that provides a vast array of statistics. You will need to get some code from Google first, though. Just visit the site, sign in with your Google Account and then sign up for Google Analytics. (For more information on Google Accounts, see "Google Services" on page 88.) Once you have been provided the necessary code, embed it in your blog. Please note that it is generally only available to self-hosted blogs, so not if yours is hosted by WordPress.com.

Tip	If you don't feel comfortable inserting this piece of code into your blog, ask your developer or a more technically savvy friend to do it for you.

You can measure such elements as:

- Visits by country.

- Bounce rate, i.e., how many people come to read just one blog post (page) and then leave.

- Visits from mobile devices.

- Which browsers are being used to view your blog.

Twitter Measurement

Now, the two tools I have mentioned above can measure traffic sources, such as Twitter, but there are a couple of other simple tools that are both useful and fun.

Tool 3: Bitly

Figure 5 Bitly stats for Jeff Bullas's shortened links

Bitly (*www.bitly.com*) measures statistics for your Bitly-shortened links on Twitter and displays elements such as:

- Which countries are clicking your shortened links on Twitter, along with their percentages.

- Which of your shortened links on Twitter are getting the most clicks.

Tool 4: Twitter Counter

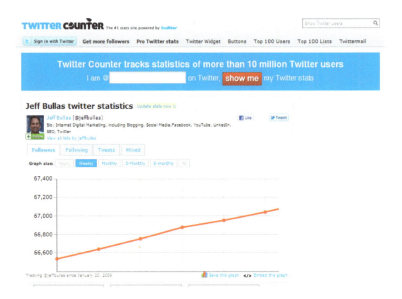

Figure 6 Twitter Counter stats for Jeff Bullas's page

Twitter Counter (*www.twittercounter.com*) is a simple tool that can provide basic statistics on your Twitter follower growth. If you buy the paid version, it will provide even more statistics to view — and chew up your time.

Facebook Measurement

Facebook and Google don't get along — and Google+ isn't helping, either — so if you want the best statistics from Facebook and want to keep track of all your Facebook figures, then you will need to use Facebook's Insights tool. This is only available to people or brands that have set up a Facebook page rather than just a personal profile, and even then only pages with at least 30 likes.

Tool 5: Facebook Insights

Figure 7 Facebook Insights stats for Jeff Bullas's page

Facebook Insights provides Facebook page owners and platform developers with content- and user-related metrics by understanding and analyzing trends within user growth, user demographics, content consumption and content creation. They are then better equipped to improve their businesses with Facebook.

There are many tools to measure your success online with your blog and social media channels, and this just touched on a few of them and some the basics. Google Analytics is by far one of the most comprehensive tools available, it's free and it should be a mandatory inclusion for any blogger or website owner.[2]

Benchmark Metrics for Budgeting

Always keep in mind the workflow that goes along with any social project; for example, a video would include:

1. Producing the video.

2. Posting it to YouTube.

3. Posting it to Facebook.

4. Writing a blog post about it and posting to the blog with an embedded YouTube video.

---

[2] 5 Tools to Measure Your Social Media Success by Jeff Bullas refer to www.jeffbullas.com

5. Posting the video and transcript to the website's video section for search engine optimization (SEO).

6. Adding it to the website's video sitemap to give search engines useful information about it.

7. Extracting 10 facts from the video and scheduling 10 Facebook posts over the next three months linking to the video.

8. Extracting 10 facts from the video and scheduling 10 posts on Twitter, or tweets, over the next three months linking to the video.

9. Optional promotional/integration tactics, such as:

    • Adding the link to the blog post (with the embedded video) to company email signatures.

    • Dropping a press release regarding the video and linking it to the blog post.

- Dropping an email regarding the video to the house list.

- Embedding the video in banner ads.

10. Measuring video plays across platforms.

11. Measuring leads and return on investment (ROI) from video visits on the blog, the website and social promotions.

If you are an organization that wishes to have a layer of brand or legal compliance, these items may need to be put into a publishing schedule so that brand managers, marketing managers or legal teams can approve the content.

For most, it can be pretty simple: Act like you're at a party that's attended by both your grandmother and your boss. Be friendly and fun but well behaved and discreet. Don't swear or reveal confidential information.[3]

---

[3] Benchmark Metrics for Budgeting – Social Media Benchmarking Q&A – Harry Gold- www.clickZ.com

Marketing Plan

On average, between creating and gathering content, writing tweets and posts, moderating and responding to comments and producing monthly reports, one could easily spend on average 30 to 90 minutes per day per Facebook page and up to 30 minutes per day on a Twitter account. Clearly, time goes as your fan and follower base grows and the frequency of posts increase. Also, this person should be looking for ways to incorporate and integrate social media into marketing programs that already exist. So 10 to 20 hours a month should be allotted to strategy and integration tactics development, as well as to special content development.

Video is always great content since it can trigger social activity — as shown by the workflow under "Benchmark Metrics for Budgeting" (page 29) — and is easy to share using Facebook- and Twitter-sharing buttons. However, it is not the only thing a company should be doing. Video should always be part of the mix along with photos, info-graphics, white papers, fact sheets, studies, checklists, coupons, articles, blog posts and other content being produced by your organization and other media outlets and bloggers.

It can also get expensive and time-consuming if you want to be pushing a steady stream of high-quality, interesting content. If you are set up with the right equipment (a basic video camera and laptop) and are willing to push low-production-value or casual video content, you can certainly up the volume and frequency of video content you push. In most cases, to successfully produce a regular and ongoing video in the style of a video blog, or blog, you need a very interesting personality or luminary who is prepared to produce regular segments.

A famous example of video blogging is Gary Vaynerchuk's Wine Library TV (*tv.winelibrary.com*). He has produced nearly a thousand videos, and while the production value of the videos is low, their informational value is very high for wine lovers. So he has a huge following and his vlog and social media tactics drive his wine business. Any company that represents a facet of life, business and consumerism can own a space by creating an ongoing stream of valuable video content. But the key here is "ongoing." Through Gary's videos, he has organically (in other words, without advertising) garnered over 35,000 Facebook fans and 850,000 Twitter followers and has generated millions of video views.

Suggested Equipment and Software Investments

These will be needed for different initiatives. If you are doing video, for instance, clearly you will want a good camcorder or webcam, a good microphone input (so that your sound is clear), video-editing software (either the basic software that comes with the recorder or something nicer like Adobe Premiere), a powerful-enough computer and, of course, a YouTube channel. Camtasia, by TechSmith, is also good for turning Microsoft PowerPoint decks into videos.

As for managing social media content production and collaboration, workflow, monitoring and measurement, there are a number of tools and technologies. There are things like HootSuite (for more information, see "HootSuite: Your Social Media Management Dashboard" on page 137) and TweetDeck that are on the lower end of the spectrum, and then there are more robust end-to-end social media management tools like the one we use that was developed by Gnowit. Depending on how in-depth your company wants to measure the levels of chatter and buzz out there around your brand, we offer a more robust program.[4]

---

[4] Benchmark Metrics for Budgeting – Social Media Benchmarking Q&A – Harry Gold- www.clickZ.com

Traditional vs. Social Media Measurement

The biggest challenge for marketers and the holders of the purse strings is proving the correlation between advertising spends and direct revenue. There is no foolproof way of proving a link unless you decide one year to do something radically different, like spend nothing or spend big on a specific season's advertising. But even then, the campaign effectiveness can be affected by prevailing market conditions. There are, however, many ways to measure the impact of campaigns.

Traditional media, such as newspapers, radio and outdoor advertising, should be measured in terms of their target audience impressions and by benchmarking the cost per thousand impressions. Remember to include the production costs as well as the media cost in calculating the cost per thousand, or CPM (cost per mille, where "mille" is Latin for "thousand"). A good advertising agency should also be able to provide reach and frequency data. Reach is the percentage of your target audience (e.g., 25- to 55-year-olds) that is exposed to your message, while frequency is the estimated number of times individuals will see your message. Frequency is vitally important, and this figure should exceed three times. Advertising only seen once or twice is rarely effective.

Historically, advertisers have used different telephone numbers on different media to establish the cost per call generated. Some channels perform much better due to the nature of the media. People are more likely to call from a piece of direct mail delivered to their home than from a 48-sheet poster that is only seen for three or four seconds. Over the last few years, there has been a noticeable decline in the number of telephone calls generated from advertising, primarily because websites are now the preferred method of contact and information search.

Personally, I don't see the difference between traditional media and social media with regard to measurement.

Digital marketing wins hands down in the battle with traditional media in terms of impact and measurability. Running Facebook campaigns or other digital advertising is highly measureable and accountable. The statistics available include the number of impressions, clickthroughs (to your website) and the cost per clickthrough. Digital marketing is contextual, namely, we can target specific audiences. For example, a million impressions for outdoor advertising are a million impressions of the entire adult population, whereas a million impressions on Facebook will be of just your bull's-eye target audience.

The effectiveness of the public relations (PR) elements of your seasonal campaign should also be measured. The best method is to use equivalent advertising spend. Just remember to include online and traditional media in coverage and all agency or staff costs. Equivalent advertising expenditure is simple, yet time-consuming to calculate. If you get half a page of editorial in the local newspaper, you simply apply the advertising value to it; hence you can calculate the advertising value of PR for each dollar of cost. Media Maverix has a system that will create these metrics for you and which can even be broken down by faculty or division and by individual news story.

Social media deployment is becoming an integral part of campaigns. Social media measurement is possible but can be quite expensive. Media Maverix runs systems to measure the volume of social nd/or traditional media activity for you and your competitors. These systems also provide audience sentiment toward your brand and how this sentiment changes over time.

Corporate Structure for Social Media Marketing

A corporate structure is essentially the layout of the various departments, divisions and job positions that interact to conduct the business of the company. Generally, a corporate structure is necessary to ensure that all important tasks are conducted according to the guidelines of the corporation, as well as to provide lines of communication and authority for the overall function of the company. Even the smallest of businesses have a corporate structure, although its exact format may be extremely simplistic.

A corporate structure usually helps to accomplish three things: First, the corporate layout helps to define all the areas of responsibility within the company. The accounting department is understood to handle all financial matters, such as paying the company's bills and issuing invoices for services rendered. The sales department works to ensure that there are efforts to market the goods and services produced to the consumer market. Provisions for executive, managerial and administrative matters are also normally accounted for in a corporate structure so that everyone in the organization knows where a given issue should be addressed.[5]

I suppose you are wondering how this translates to social media. It's simple: no well-executed plan works without structure. You just need to decide what sort of structure works for your company. Big or small, a structure needs to be determined for your social media strategy and implementation.

Networking giant Cisco has embraced this philosophy already, and it is only a matter of time before all companies follow suit. So let's get ahead of the pack, thanks to consultant Dado Van Peteghem's excellent description of Cisco's social media integration (as shown in Figure 8 below):

"At Cisco the coordinating strategy for social media is determined by a team of ten — a centre of

---

[5] WizeGEEK Q&A site: Corporate Structure

excellence. They ensure the elaboration of the general approach, write guidelines and advise. They manage the corporate social brand, gather knowledge and analyse metrics.

"The translation of the general approach for the specific target groups is done by the people responsible in each department. Their assignment is to change the standard philosophy into a local strategy for specific projects. An effective method, since they have the best knowledge of their target audience."

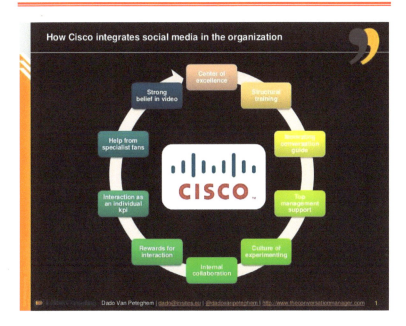

Figure 8 Cisco's social media integration

I couldn't have said it better, myself. Another example of how to add structure to your corporate social media is shown in Figure 9 below.

Corporate Structure for Social Media Marketing

Have a trained team

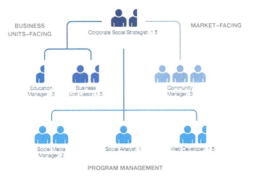

Figure 9 The composition of a social media team

For small businesses, the structure does not need to be quite so elaborate; however, a structure that considers all elements is definitely required.[6]

---

[6] Author, Dado Van Peteghem Cisco's Social Media Integration Plan"

Digital Marketing Strategy

Introduction

Digital marketing planning.

First Things First

Digital marketing planning is no different than any other marketing planning; in fact, it's increasingly strange to have separate plans for digital and offline because that's not how your customers perceive your business. However, we're often required to separate plans for digital-only based on the way teams and reporting are structured and to help the transition to digital — before it becomes business as usual. A common format helps align your plan to other marketing plans.

Some General Planning Advice

- Focus on building a plan around the customer, not your products and tactics.

- Situations and plans change, especially online, so ensure plans are usable by having a clear vision for the year and by keeping real detail to a shorter-term, 90-day focus.

- Make plans fact-based and state assumptions so that it's easy for others to buy into what you're saying.

- Keep it simple! "Jargon lite" is best. Again, this helps others buy into what you're saying.

- Keep plans up to date. (Monthly is more than enough.)

- There isn't a perfect plan; what's needed changes according to each business.

Creating the General Structure

Knowing where to start is often the hardest part of writing a digital marketing plan. But once you have a structure or framework to follow in a table of contents, it's almost a matter of filling in the gaps. At Media Maverix, we recommend the SOSTAC® — Situation Analysis, Objectives, Strategy, Tactics, Action and Control — planning structure developed by P. R. Smith, co-author (with Dave Chaffey) of *Emarketing Excellence: Planning and Optimizing your Digital Marketing*. This is a great framework for business, marketing and digital marketing plans because it's simple and logical, making it easy to remember and to explain to colleagues or agencies.

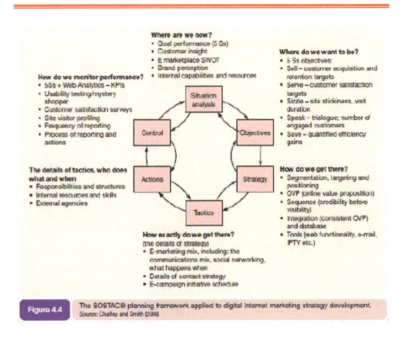

Figure 4.4 | The SOSTAC® planning framework applied to digital Internet marketing strategy development.
Source: Chaffey and Smith (2008)

Figure 10 SOSTAC® in action

Each of the six areas (as shown in Figure 10 above) helps in separating out the key strategies, such as customer acquisition, conversion and retention. In the sections that follow, headings are provided to help structure your strategy, with prompts in italics to help your thinking.

Situation Analysis

Where are we now?

Understanding your online marketplace.

The Immediate (Micro) Environment

A. Our customers.

Always start with the customer — their characteristics, behaviors, needs and wants. You should define:

- Options for segmenting and targeting: You should apply your traditional segments but also consider the new microtargeting options, such as market segmentation and direct marketing data mining (just to mention a few).

- Ideal customers: Characteristics summarized in named personas are useful to get started, but think about demographics, search behaviors, product-selection behaviors and unmet needs — detail here is very useful. See it from the customer's perspective; ask "What would John do?" and "What would Jane think?" Also consider what your data tells you in regard to your most profitable and potentially profitable customers.

B. Our market.

- Market description: Focus on actionable needs and trends — what are they, and are you meeting them? — as this insight is useful for other teams. You should find out what other teams know, what exactly is growing in the market and whether there is evidence you can draw upon.

C. Our competitors.

- Benchmark against competitors for your customer personas and scenarios using the criteria provided under "Strategy" (page 57), with emphasis on the marketing mix.

- It's also important to benchmark against competitors for key digital tactics like SEO and social media marketing. There are suggestions for this under "Benchmark for a Point of Reference" (page 20).

D. Intermediaries, influencers and potential partners.

- Review customers' use of the different types of sites that may be influencing their decisions, such as search engines, specialist news sites, aggregators, social networks and bloggers.

| Tip | You can monitor your reputation across different influencers using a variety of tools, including monitoring tools found at *www.mediamaverix.ca*. |

E. Wider (macro) environment.

These are the big-picture strategic influences. We recommend that you don't go into too much depth on these; instead, review the influence of the main macro factors for digital in the context of customer analysis and competitor benchmarking:

- **Social** – How have consumer attitudes changed?

- **Legal** – Check that your online marketing activities comply with privacy and online trading laws *before* problems arise.

- **Environment** – Is your approach ethical and sustainable?

- **Political** – Can you take advantage of any government funding schemes?

- **Technology** – Review the latest technology.

Tip	To download a copy of our digital marketing planning template, go to *www.mediamaverix.ca*.

F. Our own capabilities.

Only once you have looked outward should you turn inward and look at your own capabilities. (Looking outward is often missed.)

G. Internet-specific strengths, weaknesses, opportunities and threats (SWOT) summary.

Include a digital-channel SWOT that summarizes your online marketplace analysis findings *and* that links to strategy. In a large organization, or for a more complete summary, complete a SWOT for:

- Customer acquisition, conversion and development.

- Different brands.

- Different markets.

- Different competitors: Direct and indirect, as this helps integrate your analysis with your strategy rather than the analysis being put on the shelf and forgotten.

Objectives

Where do we want to be?
Setting useful, actionable objectives.

To help you and your colleagues look forward to the future offered by digital marketing, we recommend the following four different types of measures, a hierarchy that we feel would also benefit larger organizations:

1. Broad, top-level goals to show how the business can benefit from digital channels.

2. Mid- to long-term vision to help communicate the transformation needed in a larger organization.

3. Specific, measurable, attainable, realistic and timely (SMART) objectives to provide clear direction and commercial targets:

    • **Specific** – A specific goal addresses as many descriptor questions — who, what, when, where, why and how —

as possible. It has a greater chance of being met if a specific plan is made for its completion.

- **Measurable** – This involves deciding what will measure or determine when the goal is attained. A finish line has to be set before it can be crossed.

- **Attainable** – To properly set a goal, you must set the steps that are necessary to reach it. This scaffolding ensures that the goal is actually attainable and therefore produces motivation, in that the goal's completion has become a reality.

- **Realistic** – A goal must be set in the spirit of desiring its completion. In setting a goal, you can determine if it's realistic by asking whether you are capable of attaining it and are willing to work for it. Setting an unrealistic goal will often result in a decrease in motivation over time.

- **Timely** – Setting a time frame for the goal helps to motivate. Without an end goal, there is no set limit to help drive the goal's completion.

4. Key performance indicators (KPIs) to check that you are on track.

You should be as specific as possible with your goals. We recommend that you do the following:

- Determine what success is for you.

- Divide your goals into the key digital strategy areas of customer acquisition, conversion, development and growth. This is important to ensure that you're covering all of the areas.

- Break your goals down into short-, medium- and long-term ones.

- Align your goals with the business and marketing ones and with how you substantiate them.

- Make sure your online goals align with the organizational ones.

- Once you have completed the KPIs, go back to the big picture and define a long-term vision for how digital will help the organization grow into the future, again, aligned with the organizational vision.

Strategy

How are you going to achieve the goals?
Setting a meaningful strategy.

The key elements of digital strategy involve revisiting and aligning the main thrust of your marketing strategy in an online context. Make sure you draw from other plans; if there aren't any, use the headers below. Don't get drawn into the details at this stage — that falls under "Tactics" (page 66).

We recommend that you summarize your strategy in a table. (This provides a great summary and integrates goals with situation, strategy, tactics and measures!) But you may want to summarize the essence of some or all of the digital strategies below. How are you going to leverage the potential of digital marketing to your business, and how does that meet the objectives? This is about your approach only, not the detail.

Consider breaking it down, as well; it's often easier to explain in smaller, bite-size chunks. This also helps when it comes to tactics, which should hang from the following strategies:

A. Targeting and segmentation.

- A company's online customers have different demographic characteristics, needs and behaviors compared to its offline customers. It follows that different approaches to segmentation may be required and that specific segments may need to be selectively targeted though specific content and messaging on your site or elsewhere on the web. This capability for microtargeting is one of the biggest benefits of digital marketing.

- The specific targeting approaches to apply online, as described in this guide, include demographic, value-based, lifecycle and behavioral personalization.

B. Positioning.

- How do you position your online products and services in the customer's mind?

- Reinforcing your core proposition: How do you prove your credibility?

- Define your online value proposition. This should flow from your positioning and be what customers see immediately when they interact with you online.

- Define these in key messages for different audiences (e.g., prospects against existing customers; segments you target that have a different value).

- You need clear messaging hierarchies to effectively communicate your positioning in both online and offline media.

C. Proposition and the marketing mix.

Think about the digital marketing mix. How can you provide differential value to customers by varying the Ps online? And, of course, how do you add value through service? You will want to explain how you will modify the marketing mix, especially if you sell online; for example:

- **Product** – Can you offer a different product range online? How can you add value to products through additional content or online services?

- **Price** – Review your pricing and consider differential pricing for online products or services.

- **Place** – Identify your online distribution issues and challenges. Should you create new intermediaries or portals, or should you partner with existing sites?

- **Promotion** – Discuss the problems and opportunities of the online communications mix. These will be detailed in the acquisition and retention communications strategies.

Review approaches for online promotions and merchandising to increase sales. You may want to include exclusive promotions to support the growth of different digital channels (e.g., email, mobile, Facebook, Twitter).

- **People** – Can you use automated tools, such as a list of frequently asked questions (FAQ), to deliver web self-service, or should you provide online contact points through live chat or phone call-back?

- **Processes** – List the components of each process and understand the need to integrate them into a system.

- **Physical evidence** – Identify the digital components that give customers evidence of your credibility, such as awards and testimonials.

- **Place** – So much of marketing today is based on strategic partnerships, marketing marriages and alliances that we have added this P in as a vital ingredient in today's marketing mix.

That should give you a good idea of how to use the Ps.

D. Brand strategy.

Gaining street cred online is now paramount to success; how and where are you going to do that? Brand favorability follows credibility and trust. What do you understand will be the reasons to engage with your brand? Why would customers click through (or not)? How will you demonstrate your credibility online?

E. Online representation or presence.

This includes your own website strategy — one site versus multiple sites; subdomains, if any; the site's goals and how they will be achieved; etc. — and priorities for social presences.

F. Content and engagement strategy.

Which content will you feature to gain initial interest, support the buying process (text and rich-media product content and tools) and stickiness and promote return visits (blogs and community)? Remember to also include user-generated content, such as reviews, ratings and comments.

You will have to prioritize content types and ensure that you devote sufficient resources to the process to create quality content that helps you compete. (All effective online companies see themselves as publishers!)

G. Digital channel acquisition communications strategy.

Outline how you will acquire traffic. What are the main approaches you will use? Don't forget to consider how you drive visitors through offline media and integrated campaigns.

Key digital media channels for traffic acquisition would include:

- Search engine marketing (natural and paid).

- Social media marketing and online PR (think brand strategy).

- Partner and affiliate marketing.

- Display advertising.

- Email marketing to leads database.

H.   Digital channel conversion strategy.

How does the user experience — which depends on information architecture, page template design, merchandising, messaging and performance — help you make it easy for visitors to engage and convert?

I.   Digital channel retention communications strategy.

Often neglected, what will be the main online and offline tactics to encourage repeat visits and sales? Again, integrated campaigns involving offline touch points are crucial here.

J.   Data strategy.

What are your goals in permission marketing and data capture (what, where, how, when and why)? What tools and value-adds are you going to use? You might alternatively reference these in the conversion strategy. How do you improve the quality of your customer data across channels to help increase the relevance of your messages through personalization?

K.   Multichannel integration strategy.

How you integrate traditional and digital channels should run through every section of your strategy because it's key to your success. One way to structure this is to map customer journeys across channels as channel chains.

L.   Social media marketing strategy.

We would argue that social media marketing is part of a broader customer engagement strategy, plus brand, acquisition, conversion and retention strategies; however, many organizations are grappling with how they get value from this, so it may help to develop overall social media marketing.

M.   Digital marketing governance strategy.

In larger organizations, how you manage digital marketing is a big challenge. Questions that the governance strategy seeks to answer include how we manage internal and external resources through changes to structures and skills needed for digital and multichannel marketing.

Tactics

The details of strategy.

Tactics are where the rubber hits the road to get results, so you need to define how you will implement your strategy in the real world — when you'll do it, with what, your goals for each tactic aligned to the main objectives and how that will that be measured.

Each of strategies A to M (pages 58 to 66) will need implementation details, which you can get specialists in your team or agencies to develop. Remember that with digital, the devil is in the details. The best digital strategies can fail if the execution is poor. Search, social and email marketing and creating a persuasive web design are classic examples of this we see daily.

If there is only you, create a plan and go for it. You have the benefit of being more nimble, so you can test and learn.

How are you going to divide the year up? Thinking about campaigns versus seasonal or business focuses helps to get the plan actionable. Consider quarterly (90-day) blocks to focus on and ensure that objectives, strategies and tactics are focused on that.

Keep this section light and fact-based and avoid repeating too much description from the strategy section. Hang your tactics under the strategic hangers (e.g., traffic acquisition) so that they're easy for others to follow.

Actions and Control

Making it happen.

Create Measurable KPIs

This is to align against objectives and stay on track. Issues to reference include:

- Budgets for media, digital platform investments and resources.

- Timescales, including a longer-term roadmap if necessary.

- Organize your measuring in dashboards so that it's easy to summarize and keep up to date against the plan.

- Consider KPIs that relate to tactics, strategies and therefore objectives. Sometimes a KPI *is* an objective; for example, a KPI could be the total weekly natural search traffic, home page bounce rate or email open rate. These can be good early warnings to objectives like "online sales revenue" or "new leads" not being met. Plain old Microsoft Excel will suffice; the spreadsheet will allow you to keep the latest results to hand.

- The key is that, assuming your objectives were clear, detailed and relevant, you have the headers to site your KPIs and measure against.

- Consider how you will measure and report using web analytics.

- Are there other measurement tools and resources needed?

- What will the process measure and report? For example, looking at keyword-level traffic daily is not actionable, but home page bounce can be if site changes are made.

- Think about creating a KPI-summary dashboard.

Governance

In larger organizations, you have to think about resourcing, i.e.:

- **Skills** – Internal and agency requirements to deliver on your plan.

- **Structure** – Do you have a separate digital team, or can you integrate?

- **Systems** – The processes to make things work and keep you agile.

Executive Summary

No, you're still not quite finished. After your plan is created, go back to the beginning and create a one-page summary that a busy senior executive can understand and believe in. The same executive summary is useful for Microsoft PowerPoint presentations should you need to present the bones of your plan and the ROI. An important part of your role is helping others understand what digital marketing is and the immense value that it can add to the business. Naturally, the executive summary should contain a two-line summary of each part of SOSTAC® (challenging!) but stressing the need for investment in digital channels and showing the key issues:

1. **Situation analysis.**

   - Key issues requiring action.

2. **Objectives.**

   - Our vision.

   - Key goals.

3. **Strategy.**

   - Segmentation, targeting and positioning.

   - Brand development and customer engagement.

   - Customer acquisition.

   - Customer retention and growth.

- Reputation management.[7]

4. Tactics, actions and control.

- Investment and budget.

- Resourcing.

- Timescales.

- Success factors for managing change.

- Measurement and testing.

---

[7] Dave Chaffey and Danyl Bosomwoth – Smart Insights

How to Handle Reputation Management Online

Reputation management is as important as reputation building. There are several online tools available to help you manage your reputation, including Google Alerts, Facebook, Twitter and social media management applications like HootSuite. (These tools are covered in the section titled "A Step-by-Step Guide to Getting Started," starting on page 88.) Most platforms have a way to search for and exclude keywords, which is very useful for reputation management.

Google's results and those of other search engines are a little more difficult, though. It's nearly impossible to make a negative Google result simply disappear, although some "black hat" SEO practitioners claim to have the gift. Instead, your best approach is to provide Googlebot and other spiders (web crawlers used by search engines to index content) with a healthier diet of web content showing your reputation in a positive light.

On that note, here are our recommendations for the best web content to fill up the first page of Google's results.

1. Get your own website.

It sounds simple enough, doesn't it? Unfortunately, you'd be surprised at the number of individuals and companies that haven't registered their own branded domain name and put up a website. Registering *yourcompanyname.com* or *yourpersonalname.com* and adding a basic website is a surefire way to occupy one of the top 10 Google listings for your name.

2. Start a blog.

If you love and nurture a blog, it will likely become a great asset in your reputation-management arsenal. But the great thing about a blog is that it tends to rank well even when left unwatered. Blogs are the cactuses of online content. WordPress.com and Google-owned Blogger (*www.blogger.com*) both provide free blogs and free hosting. Just add a few posts, keep it targeted to your name — use it in the blog title, posts, etc. — throw in a few links and bake for a few days, and it'll be on the first page of Google in no time flat.

3.   Add a subdomain.

If you've put a lot of effort into growing your main website, chances are there's an opportunity to add a subdomain. Subdomains are great. Google considers them separate from your main site, but they still include your main brand. There are a lot of great reasons to add a subdomain: careers, corporate info, product info — you name it. Take a look at the Marketing Pilgrim Job Board (*jobs.marketingpilgrim.com*) for an example.

4.   Create a social networking profile.

Google+, Twitter, Facebook and other social networking profiles can rank well for your personal or company name. When you sign up, be sure to use your real name — using a nickname won't help with your Google reputation — and enable the option that lets you pick the address (the URL —

uniform resource locator) of your profile. *www.facebook.com/companyname* works a whole lot better than *www.facebook.com/12345678*.

5. Create your own social network.

If a social networking profile ranks well in Google, how much more so your own social network? Ning (*www.ning.com*) will let you create your own customized social network. For US$25 a month, you get to point your own domain name at it. Take a look at Classroom 2.0 (www.classroom20.com) for an example.

6. Create a business profile.

You should join LinkedIn (*www.linkedin.com*) because it's a great tool for networking with your peers. You should also join it because it allows you to talk about yourself, link to your other Google-friendly web content and customize your profile's address. Wouldn't you rather that your potential employer searched Google and found your LinkedIn profile than that account of the run-in you had with your last boss?

7. Share your photos.

Flickr (*www.flickr.com*) is very Google-friendly. Upload photos of you, your company's logo, your products, etc. and label them using your name. Add some comments, including your name, to each photo, and — voila! — you've just added a dozen pages of content, each one labeled with your company's name. Be sure to do the same when selecting your Flickr profile name.

8. Claim your identity.

Naymz (*www.naymz.com*) is a blessing for those looking to control their Google reputation. It effectively lets you create a profile and then link to all of your other profiles. Whereas LinkedIn is heavy on the networking side, Naymz is more of a holding tank for your brand. Best of all, Google seems to love it.

9.   Create your own wiki.

If you're facing a Google-reputation nightmare, you might be tempted to create your own Wikipedia page. After all, Wikipedia ranks all over Google, right? Bad move. Not only is it hard to get one approved but Wikipedia's volunteers are totally unbiased. And because Wikipedia's content is crowdsourced, that driving-under-the-influence (DUI) incident you're trying to cover up will likely make its way onto your page. Not good. Instead, create your own wiki and build your profile that way. Wiki software like MediaWiki (*www.mediawiki.org*) and wiki-hosting sites like Wikispaces (*www.wikispaces.com*) are perfect for this. You can focus the wiki on your name or your company's name. The best part is that you get to decide who contributes to the wiki.

10. Get a free webpage from Google.

I've saved the best for last. OK, I lied. While a free webpage from Google Sites (*sites.google.com*) isn't the best web content for managing your Google reputation, there's something satisfying about having Google help mend your reputation.

So there you have it. While none of these should be used as a get-out-of-jail-free card — you should avoid the reputation nightmare in the first place — they'll at least help you rebuild your Google reputation.[8]

---

[8] Google Reputation Management by Andy Beal at Marketingpilgrim.com

Why Have Social Responsibility?

Social responsibility has become an increasingly important and necessary part of business today. Social relevance will soon be a measurement tool used by consumers to determine whether or not they want to do business with you.

According to Wikipedia: Corporate social responsibility (CSR) has been defined by Lord Holme and Richard Watts in the World Business Council for Sustainable Development publication *Corporate Social Responsibility: Making Good Business Sense* as "the continuing commitment by business to behave ethically and contribute to economic development while improving the quality of life of the workforce and their families as well as the local community and society at large."

CSR is one of the newest management strategies, where companies try to create a positive impact on society while doing business. There is no clear-cut definition of what CSR comprises. Every company has different CSR objectives, although the main motive is the same. All companies have a two-point agenda: improving qualitatively (the management of people and processes) and improving quantitatively (the impact on society). The second is as important as the first, and company stakeholders are increasingly taking an interest in the "outer circle," i.e., the activities of the company and how these affect the environment and society.

Social responsibility is an ethical ideology or theory in which an entity, be it an organization or individual, has an obligation to act for the benefit of society at large. Social responsibility is a duty every individual or organization has to perform so as to maintain a balance between the economy and the ecosystem. A trade-off exists between economic development (in the material sense) and the welfare of the environment and society. Social responsibility means sustaining the equilibrium between the two. It pertains not only to business organizations but to anyone who's actions affect the environment. This responsibility can be passive, by avoiding engaging in socially harmful acts, or active, by performing activities that directly advance social goals.

Here are some examples of companies that have embraced social responsibility:

> **Note** The dollar amounts in this list are in Canadian dollars.

Bank of Montreal

- Accessibility initiatives have resulted in an increase in business with Aboriginal customers, from $1.4 billion in 2008 to $1.7 billion in 2010.

- It is one of two investors in the Greening Canada Fund, a first-ever carbon emissions reduction fund exclusively targeting large Canadian corporations. The fund will purchase and redistribute carbon offset credits sourced from social and nonprofit organizations.

- In March 2011, the company launched the BMO Eco Smart Mortgage at a market-leading rate, making it more accessible to mainstream customers.

Gap Inc.

- In 2011, the International Center for Research on Women (ICRW) named Gap the recipient of the Champions for Change Award for Innovation in recognition of its Personal Advancement and Career Enhancement program, which provides life skills and enhanced technical skills to female garment workers to help them advance in the workplace.

- To implement company-wide environmental initiatives, it has formed an environmental council comprised of senior executives and mid-level managers.

Loblaw Companies Limited

- Organic waste collected from select corporate stores in Ontario are sent to biogas facilities to generate renewable energy, while eight Quebec stores send their organic waste to local farms to be converted into compost material.

- Loblaw's Grown Close to Home program promotes local Canadian growers. Approximately 40 percent of produce in Loblaw stores is locally sourced during July and August.

- Loblaw has a goal to reduce nonrecyclable packaging in its own control-brand products by 50 percent by year-end 2013. Between 2007 and 2011, the company also reduced the number of shopping bags from its stores by 2.5 billion and, in 2010, reported a 73 percent reduction in shopping-bag use Canada-wide.

PepsiCo

- PepsiCo Canada achieved 98 percent waste diversion from landfill and 40 percent water-usage reduction at its manufacturing plants.

- The company was the first manufacturer in Canada to introduce all-electric, zero-emissions, green-powered delivery trucks into its distribution network.

- It spent over $1 billion globally in 2009, alone, supporting minority- and women-owned businesses in its supply chain.

Starbucks Corporation

- It is a founding member of Business for Innovative Climate and Energy Policy (BICEP), a coalition of companies that advocates for stronger clean-energy and climate-change regulations.

- Through the provision of its Youth Action Grants, Starbucks engaged 53,736 young people in 2010 to take actions that benefited their communities.

- It increased investments to promote the awareness and use of its reusable-tumbler discount program, which kept 1.45 million lb. of paper out of landfills in 2010.

And that's just to name a few. There are now many companies embracing social responsibility. It is something you should be thinking about, as it will lead to your social relevance.

Why Is Social Relevance Important?

There are independent, third-party companies that are going to be evaluating your social relevance online. You will basically have a score associated with your name or company based on your activity online.

Your social relevance score will have an impact on who will want to work with you. Consumers will be apprehensive to work with companies that do not have social relevance scores.

The faster you understand how the technology works and get on board, the faster your relevance will start building.

This is something to consider moving forward.

A Step-by-Step Guide to Getting Started

Note	Social media sites often change their layouts, so the positions of buttons, links and other parts of the user interface may be different than indicated in this guide.

Google Services

To use Google+ and most other Google services, you must first have a Google Account, i.e., a Gmail address (*username@gmail.com*). This serves as your login for any Google service that requires you to be signed in.

Figure 11 Signing in to Google to sign up

If you don't already have a Google Account, on the Google home page (*www.google.com* or your localized version), click the **Sign in** button in the upper-right corner (as shown in Figure 11 above) and then, on the **Google Accounts** page, click the **SIGN UP** button.

Google+

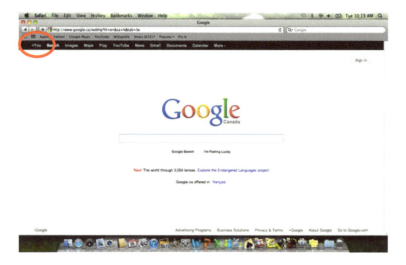

Figure 12 Google+ is +You

Google+ is Google's social network, launched in June 2011. As of September 2012, it has 400 million users. To access Google+, in the navigation bar, click **+You** (as shown in Figure 12 above) or, if you're already signed in, **+Name**.

Tip	Google's navigation bar, the current — black — version of which debuted in 2011, is available on several of the company's sites, not just its home page.

Your Google+ Home Page

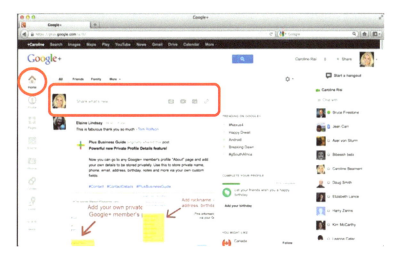

Figure 13 Your Google+ home page

Your Google+ home page — in the sidebar, click the **Home** button (as shown in Figure 13 above) — is where you see your stream which contains the posts shared by people and businesses in your circles. This is also where you will go to create your posts using the **Share what's new...** box (see Figure 13). Creating your own content is important — don't only share links and other people's posts. It's also important to interact with people in your circles. You can make circles for employees, clients, family — anything you want — and speak directly to just that audience or to everyone at once.

Your Google+ Profile

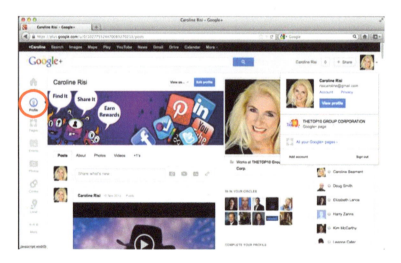

Figure 14 Your Google+ profile

To create a Google+ business page, you first need to set up a personal Google+ profile from which to manage your business page. To set up your profile, in the sidebar, click the **Profile** button (as shown in Figure 14 above). From there you can decide whether or not you're going to complete the full personal profile and actually use it. Visitors to your business page will not know that it is connected to this personal profile. Keep in mind that creating an active and engaging personal profile can be a way to further promote your page and business.

In fact, because Google ranks content generated through its services higher than content originating elsewhere, Google+ can be useful for boosting the SEO ranking for all your Internet products.

Completing your profile in its entirety using business-relevant and keyword-rich content, including links to your website, is one way to use Google+ to improve your SEO. The more +1s you get, and the more people who add your business page to their circles, the better it is for your ranking.

Creating Your Google+ Business Page

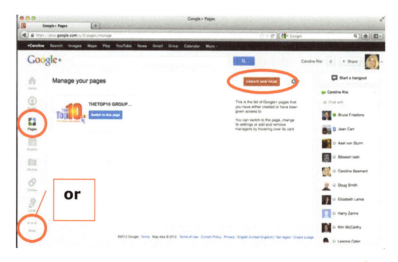

Figure 15 Managing your Google+ pages

To set up a Google+ business page, in the sidebar, click the **Pages** button (as shown in Figure 15 above). If it's not there point to the **More** button and then drag the **Pages** button to the sidebar. (The buttons in the sidebar can be dragged into whatever order you prefer and unneeded ones can be dragged to the **More** button.) On this page you will see any pages you already manage as well as the **CREATE NEW PAGE** button (see Figure 15).

Click it and then click the category that best suits your business — **Local Business or Place**; **Product or Brand**; **Company, Institution or Organization**; **Arts, Entertainment or Sports**; **Other** — and fill in your company's information.

Tip:	If you do not have a graphic designer to create your social media image or design, be sure to hire a company that understands your business goals and which can implement a continuity of design. Visit _www.mediamaverix.ca_.

Managing Your Google+ Business Page

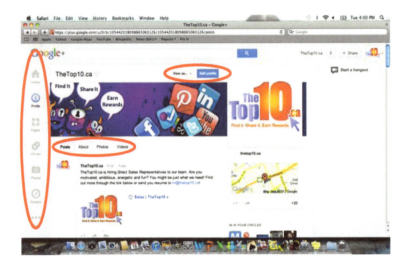

Figure 16 Google+ options to manage your page

To manage the page you created for your business, in the sidebar, click the **Pages** button (as shown in Figure 16 above) and then, on the **Manage your pages** page, click the **Switch to this page** button corresponding to your business's page. Whenever you switch to a page and are using Google+ as a page instead of as your personal profile, the following message is displayed along the top of the page until you click **OK**: "You are now using Google+ as the *Page Name* page."

To navigate the different elements of Google+ when using a page, use the sidebar and the buttons on the page itself. To see how your page appears to others, at the top of it, click the **View as...** button (see Figure 16) and then either enter a user's name to see how it appears to that user or click **Public** to see how it appears to the public. To edit the profile associated with your page, at the top of it, click the **Edit profile** button (see Figure 16).

Uploading Photos and Creating Albums

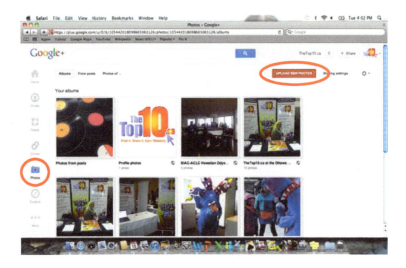

Figure 17 Your photo albums on Google+

To add a photo album to Google+, in the sidebar, point to the **Photos** button (as shown in Figure 17 above) and then click the **+ ADD PHOTOS** button. You can also click the **Photos** button and then, on the **Photos** page, click the **Upload new photos** button. All of your previously uploaded photos are displayed by source starting with those that have been instantly uploaded from your smartphone using the Google+ app. To change the source, click either the **Albums**, **From posts** or **Photos of you** button (and then click the **Instant Upload** button to go back). When you upload new photos you're given the option to create a new album for them or to add them to an existing album.

Tip	Photos are generally the most engaging type of social media content. You may want to take advantage of this by uploading interesting or visually appealing images related to your business.

Google Alerts

According to the search giant, "Google Alerts are email updates of the latest relevant Google results (web, news, etc.) based on your queries." They can be a key resource when it comes to finding news articles, blog posts and other web content related to your business and topics of interest. Not only do the alerts allow you to monitor interesting events, industry-related news and what's being said about you or your business (assisting with your reputation management), they can supply you with interesting content for your social media sites.

Figure 18 Where to find Google Alerts

To access Google Alerts, in the navigation bar, click **More** and then click **Even more** (as shown in Figure 18 above).

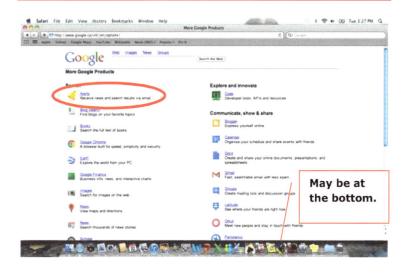

Figure 19 Google's list of products

Take a moment to go through the list on the **Products** page (as shown in Figure 19 above). The products listed there offer a tremendous number of features and benefits that can enhance your user experience and performance. To continue on to Google Alerts, scroll down and click **Alerts** (see Figure 19).

Alternately, you can go straight to *www.google.com/alerts*. (Walking you through the menu navigation was a way to make you aware of Google's other products.)

Creating and Managing Your Alerts

Figure 20 Creating a Google Alert

To create a Google Alert, in the **Search query** box (as shown in Figure 20 above), type the keywords you're interested in receiving an alert for, be they related to a specific topic, your name, your company's name, your competitor's name, an industry term, etc. Below that is where you set your preferences regarding the type of results to receive, how often to receive them, how many to receive and where they should be delivered. When you're done, click the **CREATE ALERT** button.

To view and manage this alert and any others you have created, click the **Manage your alerts** button. Although you do not need to sign in or even have a Gmail address to create alerts — any email address will do —you do have to sign in to your Google Account to manage them.

Google Places for Business

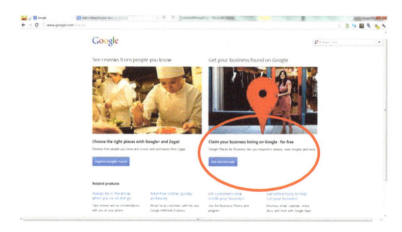

Figure 21 Connecting with Google Places for Business

Don't forget to claim your business listing on Google Places for Business (as shown in Figure 21 above). This will allow you to verify the accuracy of and add to the information (e.g., location, contact information, hours of operation) and content (including photos and videos) associated with your business on Google and Google Maps. Making sure your location is represented the way you want it to be is a key feature of the service.

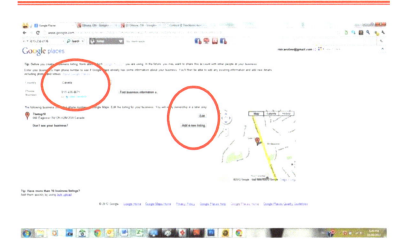

Figure 22 Adding information to Google Places for Business

It's important, it's easy and it's free. Just go to *www.google.com/placesforbusiness*, sign in to your Google Account and follow the instructions (as shown in Figure 22 above).

Facebook

Figure 23 Signing up for Facebook

Facebook (*www.facebook.com*) is a social media powerhouse. It is the largest social media site boasting a billion users (as of October 2012) many of whom are very active on the site. If you want to go where people are Facebook is a good choice in social media networks.

Tip	When building your networks, it is important to keep your demographic and geographic targets in mind.

Your Facebook Home Page

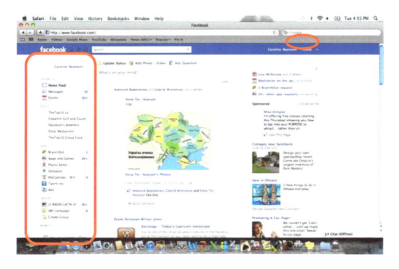

Figure 24 Your Facebook Home Page

Your Facebook home page — in the navigation bar, click **Home** (as shown in Figure 24 above) — is where you can see a stream of posts from your friends (i.e., people you have added as friends using the **Add Friend** button) and pages you've liked (i.e., pages you've clicked the **Like** button on and have therefore become a fan of). It also contains the sidebar from which you will be able to access all your pages (see Figure 24).

Your Facebook Profile

Figure 25 Your Facebook profile

Like with Google+, you will need to create a personal profile (as shown in Figure 25 above) before you can create a page for your business. It is up to you whether you do anything with this profile beyond using it to manage your business page. In terms of functionality, you manage your profile in essentially the same way as you do your business page.

Tip   Your Google+ profile photo will work as your Facebook profile picture and Twitter photo; there's no need to have a different one for each profile (unless you want to).

Creating a Facebook Page

There are two ways to create a page on Facebook.

Option 1

Figure 26 Creating a Facebook page (option 1)

On your home page, scroll down to the bottom of the right-hand column (if it isn't already visible); in the list of links below the Facebook copyright, click **More** and then click **Create a Page** (as shown in

Figure 26 above). This link is also displayed at the very bottom of your home page.

Option 2

Figure 27 Creating a Facebook page (option 2)

On any existing page — i.e., not a personal profile — click the **Create Page** button in the upper-right corner (as shown in Figure 27 above).

The Next Step

Figure 28 Selecting a category for your business

Once you have gone either of these routes, click the category that best suits your business — **Local Business or Place**; **Company, Organization or Institution**; **Brand or Product**; **Artist, Band or Public Figure**; **Entertainment**; **Cause or Community** — and fill in your company's information (as shown in Figure 28 above). Of the six categories, the first three are the most relevant to business, with **Brand or Product** being used to focus on specific products offered by a company.

Your Business's Page

Figure 29 Managing your page

The page you create for your business will look very similar to a personal profile, except for the Admin Panel at the top of the page. This is for advanced management of your page and is where notifications, messages and other information is displayed. The panel, and its content, is only visible to you — the page's administrator — and only when you are signed in. To hide the panel from (your) view click the **Hide** button at the top of the page. To show the panel when it is hidden, click the **Show** button (as shown in Figure 29 above). If the panel is not hidden, but you have scrolled below it, click the floating **Admin Panel** button.

Creating Interactions with Questions

Figure 30 Creating a question for fans to answer

Facebook gives you the option to ask questions of your page's fans. A question can be in the form of a poll, answered using the list of options you provide. You can use this feature to gather information from your page's fans and, in doing so, create interactions with them. To pose a question, on the left side of your page, click **Event, Milestone +** and then click **Question** (as shown in Figure 30 above). To make your question a poll, click **Add Poll Options**.

There are many other Facebook features for you to explore. We will be elaborating on them in Volume II. (For more information on the second volume, see page 157.)

Twitter

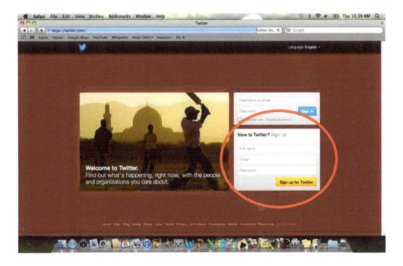

Figure 31 Signing up for Twitter

Twitter (*www.twitter.com*) is a highly engaged and active social media network. With 500 million users (as of June 2012) it offers you a great way to connect with your customers, generate leads and do reputation management.

> **Tip**   When you sign up for Twitter, try to get your company name as your username (which appears as "@username").

Your Twitter Home Page

Figure 32 Your Twitter home page

Once you sign in, you're on the Twitter home page (see Figure 32 above). It displays all the tweets from the people you follow. If you are just starting out, Twitter will give you some suggestions on who to follow. I recommend you find some of your clients (if you know who they are) or friends to get started.

Your Twitter Profile

Figure 33 Viewing your profile and tweets

Your profile is the representation of your business on Twitter. (To see how your profile appears to other users, in the navigation bar, click **Me**.) It is important that you fill out your profile in such a way as to be eye-catching and representative of your brand. Completing a short bio, adding a photo (this can be your logo), giving your location, listing your website and creating a custom background are all ways you can make your profile stand out.

To make these changes, in the navigation bar, click the gear icon and then click **Edit your profile**. If you're already on the **Me** page, just click the **Edit your profile** button in the upper-right corner (as shown in Figure 33 above).

Creating Tweets

Figure 34 Composing a tweet

To create a tweet, in the navigation bar, click the **Compose new Tweet** button and then, in the **What's happening?** pop-up window, type the text of your tweet (as shown in Figure 34 above). You can add links, an image and even your location, to your tweet. Keep in mind that tweets can only be a maximum of 140 characters long. The number at the bottom of the pop-up window indicates how many characters you have left (see Figure 34). Feel free to use abbreviations when tweeting; this is acceptable on Twitter because of the character limit.

Direct Messages

Figure 35 Viewing your direct messages

According to Twitter, "A direct message is a personal tweet seen only by the sender and the recipient." Think of it as Twitter's equivalent to email. To view your direct messages, or DMs, in the navigation bar, click the gear icon and then click **Direct messages** (as shown in Figure 35 above). The **Direct messages** pop-up window is where you can message other Twitter users privately, provided that they follow you. Should you wish to send a message containing any confidential or sensitive information or simply do not want the message to be seen publicly, be sure to use a DM rather than a tweet. It is important to keep on top of incoming DMs because existing or potential customers may reach out to you there.

Lists

Figure 36 Creating a list

Twitter lists can be a very powerful tool. (In the navigation bar, click the gear icon and then click **Lists**.) Twitter allows you to create up to 20 lists to which you can add other users. Using lists permits you to quickly see what specific groups of people are saying, as each list only shows the tweets of its members. You can make lists for such groups as clients, local media, competitors, organizations that are useful for your business to follow and interesting or popular Twitterers.

This organizational tool can help you see what different segments of people are talking about in addition to helping you filter your feed. Lists can be public or private. Because users can view and subscribe to public lists, they give you and your business the opportunity to publicly recognize others, simply by adding them to lists of your own (e.g., "Social Media Influencers," "Marketing Trendsetters").

Hashtags

A hashtag is a word or phrase, without spaces, with the hash symbol ("#") prefixed to it: "#thisisahashtag." It can be one of the most powerful tools on Twitter, in that hashtagging a word or phrase — prefixing the "#" to it — creates a live link to other tweets that contain the same hashtag. When you click the link, you're shown the top tweets containing that hashtag, starting with the most recent. You can then choose to view all of the tweets or just the ones from people you follow.

Figure 37 A hashtag in action

Using hashtags allows you to expand or focus your reach, including geographically (right down to the neighborhood or street e.g., "#Ottawa," "#Glebe," "#BankStreet"). You can also generate leads by hashtagging your company, products or services (e.g., "#MediaMaverix," "#Ottawamarketing"). By using hashtags that are relevant to your business, you can reach out to people who seek out those hashtags; for example, a restaurant in Kanata could target the lunchtime crowd with "#lunchKanata." Using hashtags of keywords or phrases related to your tweet (e.g., "#socialmedia," "#technology"), events you have a connection to (e.g., "#Winterlude," "#OttawaJazzFest"), your location (e.g., "#Ottawa," "#Toronto") — I think you get the idea — allows you to reach people who aren't following you but who may choose to now that they've seen your tweets.

Settings

Figure 38 Changing your Twitter settings

To change your Twitter settings, in the navigation bar, click the gear icon and then click **Settings** (as shown in Figure 38 above).

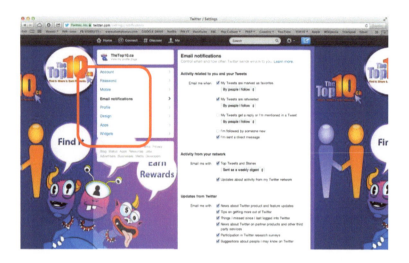

Figure 39 The sidebar on the Settings page

Use the sidebar on the **Settings** page (as shown in Figure 39 above) to change different aspects of your Twitter account.

Email Notifications

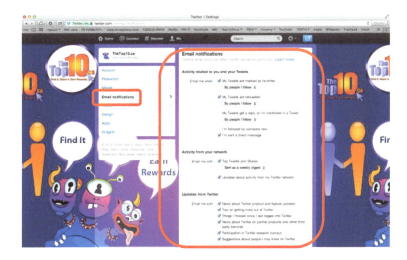

Figure 40 Email notifications

One important setting is for email notifications. (On the **Settings** page, in the sidebar, click **Email notifications**.) This setting determines when you're to receive email regarding your Twitter account. This can be a good way for you to be alerted when other people interact with your account. You can set the system to email you whenever you're sent a Direct Message, you get retweeted, one of your tweets is marked as a favorite, someone new follows you or you get a reply or mention (often referred to as an "@reply" or "@mention"). You can also receive digests related to your network and various types of updates from Twitter itself (as shown in Figure 40 above).

Connect

Figure 41 Connecting with others

You also have a Connect page — in the navigation bar, click **Connect** (as shown in Figure 41 above) — where you can see all your mentions, retweets and other interactions people have had with your account, including following you. As with direct messages, it is important to keep on top of these so that you know when someone is trying to reach out to you.

Discover

Figure 42 Discovering in Twitter

The Discover page — in the navigation bar, click **Discover** (as shown in Figure 42 above) — highlights content you might find interesting, or, as Twitter puts it, "What's happening now, tailored for you." It's based in part on tweets that are popular among the people you follow and the people they follow.

Search

Figure 43 Searching in Twitter

You can search for content by both keyword and hashtag using the **Search** box in the navigation bar (as shown in Figure 43 above). For an example of search results, specifically those for a hashtag, see Figure 37 on page 125.

One way we suggest you use the search feature is to look for your own business. Doing this allows you to see what others are saying about you, which you can then acknowledge, either by thanking them for their praise or by addressing their dissatisfaction (it is to your benefit to do so promptly).

Tips on Who to Follow

Twitter has implemented what it calls "technical follow limits." Basically, you can only follow a finite number of users, both per day and in total. This is how Twitter puts it: "Every account can follow 2,000 users total. Once you've followed 2,000 users, there are limits to the number of additional users you can follow. This number is different for each account and is based on your ratio of followers to following; this ratio is not published. Follow limits cannot be lifted by Twitter and everyone is subject to limits, even high profile and [application programming interface] accounts."

With that in mind, you will want to strategically select who to follow. Here are our suggestions:

- Follow active and engaged users. Users who are not active are not as useful to you. They are less likely to see your tweets (much less share them) or interact with you on Twitter.

- Find local influencers. Users from your area, who use Twitter religiously, can be great resources. Their tweets can help keep you abreast of what's going on and engaging with them does wonders for relationship building.

- Follow industry-related Twitter accounts, such as those of advice providers, public figures and bloggers. These may end up being useful contacts, sources of trade tips or other resources you can use.

- Though it may be tempting to follow users who advertise that they will "follow back," few, if any, of these users are valuable to your business. They usually only want a large number of followers for the sake of having a large number of followers. They are unlikely to actually care about, or engage meaningfully with, your business.

- You will probably also *not* want to follow:

  o Users who use vulgar/profane language or who are aggressive/abusive toward other users.

  o Spammers — users who tweet nothing but spam and spam links (e.g., "Hello somebody is spreading terrible rumors about you http://bit.ly/... [i.e., shortened URL]"; "I lost 20 pounds in 5 days with this, YOU can too! http://bit.ly/...").

HootSuite: Your Social Media Management Dashboard

Figure 44 Signing up for HootSuite

HootSuite (*www.hootsuite.com*) is a social media tool you can use to monitor and schedule posts on

Facebook, Google+, Twitter, LinkedIn, Foursquare and other platforms. This will save you time when engaging with your social networks.

Your Streams

Figure 45 Your streams in HootSuite

The Streams page acts as your home page. (In the sidebar, click the **Streams** button.) With HootSuite, you can view streams of content from different social networks simultaneously. This means you can monitor what's happening on all your connected networks, all in one place. You can even add streams for Twitter keyword or hashtag searches. Your social networks are displayed as tabs along the top of the page (as shown in Figure 45 above). Click these tabs to switch between the networks.

Your Social Networks

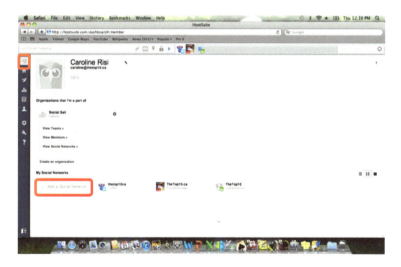

Figure 46 Your social networks in HootSuite

To add a social network to your HootSuite dashboard, at the top of the sidebar, click your profile image (or, if you haven't uploaded one yet, HootSuite's owl logo). Your social networks, along with the **Add a Social Network** button, are displayed below your profile (as shown in Figure 46 above).

Tip	The expanding sidebar along the left side of the page is referred to by HootSuite as the Launch Bar, but you will likely only see the term if you consult HootSuite Help.

A HootSuite Free account can hold a maximum of five social networks, while a HootSuite Pro (paid) account can hold more and comes with expanded analytics. The upgrade is not terribly expensive on a monthly basis; depending on how diligent you become with your social interactions, it may be well worth the investment.

Scheduled Posts

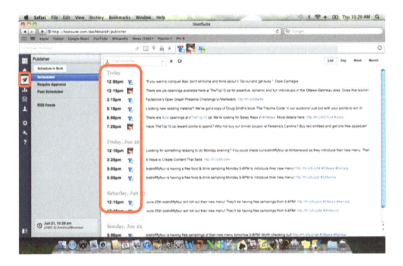

Figure 47 Scheduled posts in HootSuite

Your HootSuite dashboard also allows you to schedule posts to be sent out to selected networks at a later date and time. The Publisher page — in the sidebar, click the **Publisher** button — displays all the messages that have already been prepared, starting with those that are currently scheduled (as shown in Figure 47 above). To view the messages that are awaiting approval, click **Require Approval**. To view the ones that are already past their scheduled dates and times (i.e., they've been sent), click **Past Scheduled**. To go back to the ones that are ready to go, click **Scheduled**.

Creating and Scheduling Posts

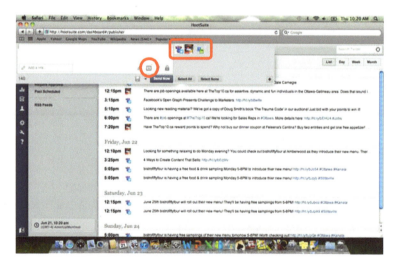

Figure 48 Creating and scheduling posts in HootSuite

To create a post: click the **Compose Message...** box at the top of the screen and then, with the cursor flashing in the now-expanded box, type your message. You can then add links, attach an image or file and add your location to your post. To the right of the box are your social networks in icon form. Click and select the icons of the networks you want the post to be sent to; these will now have green check marks.

HootSuite sends posts immediately by default hence the **Send Now** button. To schedule a post for the future, in lower-right corner of the **Compose Message...** box, click the **Scheduling** button — the "30" — and then choose the day and time you would like the post to be sent. With HootSuite Free you will need to do this individually, however, HootSuite Pro allows you to schedule multiple dates and times for your posts.

Summary

1. Social Media is the Vehicle, Not the Destination

"We often approach social media like it's the destination rather than the vehicle," said Hal Thomas, a content manager at BFG Communications, speaking at the Direct Marketing Association's 2011 conference (DMA2011). Marketers often want to "be on Twitter," but they don't consider that it's actually a communications tool and that consistent action must be taken to engage a following.

Thomas compared measuring social media ROI to the task of calculating the ROI of a business card. Conference attendees rack up hundreds of business cards, but how do you calculate the ROI of all of the business cards that you hand out at a conference?

Like a Facebook fan or Twitter follower, a business card merely represents potential, so you can't accurately measure the ROI of one, just as you can't measure the value of a Facebook fan, said Thomas.

This concept shouldn't seem new, though, because traditional marketing, such as email marketing and telemarketing, runs by these rules, Thomas explained. Marketers don't ask, "What's the ROI of this email newsletter?" Instead, they ask, "What's the conversion rate for our email campaign?" And telemarketers don't ask, "What's the ROI of a phone call?" They ask, "What's the conversion rate of our sales calls?"

Social media should be treated the same way. "You can't just ask, 'What's the ROI of social media?'" said Thomas. "You have to ask, 'What's the ROI of specific activities that we engage in via social media?'"

Thomas noted, "[Social media] is not the stopping place. It's the starting place. [Marketers] have to take action on their prospects — [they] have to take their fans and turn them from passive fans to transacting customers."

2. Listen and Apply Learnings to Every Department

Thomas advised brands to listen to the conversations generated via their social channels and learn how those discussions can benefit every department in the organization.

Thomas also gave a great example revolving around a celebrity chef whose Facebook page had accumulated more than a million fans: Each time the chef posted on Facebook, his posts generated an average of 2,000 likes and 600 comments. The chef came to Thomas asking if these numbers were "good."

Pure numbers don't say much, though. A more interesting finding, Thomas explained, would be to compare interaction levels on each post to find that the chef's followers respond in higher volume when he posts about chicken recipes and much lower volume when he posts about fish recipes. This data, if tracked over time, could be handy information for deciding what types of recipes to include in the chef's next book, for instance. In this example, it would make sense to include more chicken recipes and less fish recipes. This should translate to a more successful book, and it further extends the usefulness of social media measurement beyond the sales and marketing departments.

3. Performance Metrics Are Media Agnostic

When measuring social media success, a business must first understand how social media is being used within the organization. It is important to understand which departments are using social media and then measure success based on performance metrics that are relevant to each of those departments.

Measuring the amount of growth in Facebook fans and Twitter followers isn't going to cut it. Instead, brands should be measuring effectiveness the same way they measure success in offline activities. Thomas pointed to Olivier Blanchard's book *Social Media ROI: Managing and Measuring Social Media Efforts in Your Organization* in explaining that KPIs are media agnostic.

Summary

"It doesn't matter whether you have a billboard, a magazine ad, an online banner ad or a social media channel. Impressions are impressions," said Thomas. And that extends to all kinds of KPIs.

Sales teams run on specific metrics, while customer service departments operate on an entirely different system. Each department's success measurements for social media should be based on their specific goals and metrics.

Copyright Acknowledgments

Grateful acknowledgment is made to the following for permission to reprint and adapt previously published material:

Herein   **Source**

"   Doug Smith DSEnetwork.com

The History of the
Internet" (page 6)

Copyright Acknowledgments

Entry for 2012 (page 10) in "	Brafton Editorial, "Social marketing reaches 20 percent of the world's population," Brafton, 20 March 2012, *www.brafton.com/news/social-marketing-reaches-20-percent-of-the-worlds-population* (accessed 29 November 2012).
The History of the Internet"	
Sections on Steve Case (page 11), Ryan Ozimek (page 12) and Dries Buytaert (page 12), including their photos	Sarah Kessler, "6 Web Pioneers on What the Internet of the Future Will Look Like," Mashable, 12 January 2011, *www.mashable.com/2011/01/12/future-of-the-internet* (accessed 29 November 2012).
Section on Steve Jobs (page 13)	Evan Niu (of The Motley Fool), "Steve Jobs on Choosing Future Technologies," DailyFinance, 22 June 2012, *www.dailyfinance.com/2012/06/22/steve-jobs-on-choosing-future-technologies* (accessed 29 November 2012).

"Benchmark Metrics for Budgeting" (page 29), "Marketing Plan" (page 32) and "Suggested Equipment and Software Investments" (page 34)

Harry Gold, "Social Media Benchmarking Q&A," ClickZ, 29 March 2011, *www.clickz.com/clickz/column/2037 875/social-media-benchmarking* (accessed 29 November 2012).

"Traditional vs. Social Media Measurement" (page 36)

John Wilford, "Measuring advertising effectiveness," FE News, 19 September 2011, *www.fenews.co.uk/featured-article/measuring-advertising-effectiveness* (accessed 29 November 2012).

"Corporate Structure for Social Media Marketing" (page 40)

WiseGEEK (writing credit: Malcolm Tatum; editing credit: Bronwyn Harris), s.v. "What is Corporate Structure?," *www.wisegeek.com/what-is-corporate-structure.htm* (accessed 2 December 2012).

Copyright Acknowledgments

Dado Van Peteghem quotation (page 88), including Figure 8 (page 43)	Dado Van Peteghem, "How Cisco successfully integrates social media into their organisation," Conversation Management, 12 April 2011, *www.theconversationmanager.com/ 2011/04/12/how-cisco-successfully-integrates-social-media-into-their-organisation* (accessed 29 November 2012).
Figure 9 (page 44)	Altimeter, "Accelerating your Social Strategy to Performance" (keynote by Jeremiah Owyang, Expion: Racing Ahead 2012, Raleigh, 11 September 2012), *www.slideshare.net/jeremiah_owya ng/expion-keynote-accelerating-your-social-strategy-to-performance* (accessed 2 December 2012).
"Digital Marketing Strategy" (page 45), including Figure 10 (page 48)	Dr. Dave Chaffey and Danyl Bosomworth, "Digital marketing strategy: Planning Template," Smart Insights, June 2011 (version 2.0), *www.scribd.com/doc/28225632/v1-1-Digital-Marketing-Plan-Template* (accessed 2 December 2012).

SMART description (page 54)	Dr. Olenka Bilash, "SMART Goal Setting," Best of Bilash: Improving Second Language Education (University of Alberta Faculty of Education), May 2009, *www2.education.ualberta.ca/staff/ol enka.Bilash/best%20of%20bilash/S MART%20goals.html* (accessed 2 December 2012).
"How to Handle Reputation Management Online" (page 73)	Andy Beal, "Google Reputation Management: Fix Your Google Reputation & Remove Negative Results," Marketing Pilgrim, 31 October 2007, *www.marketingpilgrim.com/2007/10 /google-reputation-management.html* (accessed 29 November 2012).
"Why Have Social Responsibility?" (page 80)	Mallen Baker, "Corporate social responsibility - What does it mean?," Mallenbaker.net, 8 June 2004, *www.mallenbaker.net/csr/definition. php* (accessed 1 December 2012). Wikipedia, s.v. "Social responsibility," *en.wikipedia.org/wiki/Social_respon sibility* (accessed 2 December 2012).

Copyright Acknowledgments

Volume II

The second volume of the *1,2,3-Social Media Field Guide* covers an intermediate program for your social networking, including LinkedIn, Foursquare and TabSite for Facebook.

The Author

 Originally from Edinburgh, Scotland, **Caroline Risi** immigrated to Canada in 1965. Later she moved to Canada's capital to study visual arts at the University of Ottawa. She soon branched out into marketing management and has since spent the better part of her adult life building an outstanding business career.

As an Entrepreneur and Founder/CEO of THETOP10 GROUP CORP. Caroline gained over 25 years of marketing and design experience, and has taught at Algonquin College as a part-time professor.

Starting in 2009, Caroline got the urge to expand further into online solutions. She began development on a cutting-edge social business directory and network that would allow users to find the top 10 of anything anywhere in Canada.

With extensive experience in traditional and online marketing, Caroline brings a consumer's perspective and strategic plan to online marketing management and social marketing. She also offers a unique training perspective that minimizes online efforts while maximizing impact. With continuity of design and language, she reaches target audiences and effectively inspires an interactive environment, something that is key in today's market.

Contact:
Caroline@thetop10.ca